Compositions
for Recorder

Matthew Leigh EMBLETON (b1978)

Copyright ©2020 Matthew Leigh Embleton. All rights reserved.

Compositions for Recorder

Op 01 Journey in d-minor...4
Op 02 Nocturnes in d-minor and e-minor 5
Op 03 From Depth in a-minor...7
Op 04 Nocturnes in f-minor and g-minor 8
Op 05 Small Floating Crafts in c-minor..10
Op 06 Journey in a-minor...13
Op 07 Journey in c-minor...16
Op 08 Nocturne in c-minor...20
Op 10 Extransience in d-minor...22
Op 11 Victoria Park, December 2005 in e-minor (Version 2) 23
Op 12 Late Night Sky in g-minor..24
Op 13 Introduction in g-minor..26

Acknowledgments

Thanks to Michael Piraner for your collaboration, feedback, support, encouragement, friendship, and your fantastic recordings.

Thanks to the special people in my life who have supported and encouraged me in my work. Thank you for believing in me. You know who you are.

Matthew Leigh Embleton (b1978) Compositions for Recorder

Op 01 Journey in d-minor

01 Introduction, *piano con affetto*

02 The Pursuit, *con affetto e un poco agitato*

03 Looking Skyward, *con larghezza*

©2012, 2013, 2015, and 2020 Matthew Leigh Embleton

Matthew Leigh Embleton (b1978) Compositions for Recorder

Op 02 Nocturnes in d-minor and e-minor

01 Nocturne in d-minor, *piano molto e cantabile*

©2012, 2013, 2015, and 2020 Matthew Leigh Embleton

Matthew Leigh Embleton (b1978) Compositions for Recorder

02 Nocturne in e-minor, *piano molto e cantabile*

©2012, 2013, 2015, and 2020 Matthew Leigh Embleton

Matthew Leigh Embleton (b1978) Compositions for Recorder

Op 03 From Depth in a-minor

Piano molto e penseroso

©2012, 2013, 2015, and 2020 Matthew Leigh Embleton

Matthew Leigh Embleton (b1978) Compositions for Recorder

Op 04 Nocturnes in f-minor and g-minor

01 Nocturne in f-minor, *piano molto e cantabile*

02 Nocturne in g-minor (Version 1), *piano molto e cantabile (Alto Recorder in G)*

©2012, 2013, 2015, and 2020 Matthew Leigh Embleton

Matthew Leigh Embleton (b1978) Compositions for Recorder

02 Nocturne in g-minor (Version 2), *piano molto e cantabile*

©2012, 2013, 2015, and 2020 Matthew Leigh Embleton

Matthew Leigh Embleton (b1978) — Compositions for Recorder

Op 05 Small Floating Crafts in c-minor

01 Introduction, *con rubato e improvvisazione*

©2012, 2013, 2015, and 2020 Matthew Leigh Embleton

Matthew Leigh Embleton (b1978) — Compositions for Recorder

02 Interlude, *con rubato e improvvisazione* (Alto Recorder in F)

©2012, 2013, 2015, and 2020 Matthew Leigh Embleton

Matthew Leigh Embleton (b1978) — Compositions for Recorder

03 Conclusion, *con rubato e improvvisazione*

©2012, 2013, 2015, and 2020 Matthew Leigh Embleton

Matthew Leigh Embleton (b1978) — Compositions for Recorder

Op 06 Journey in a-minor

01 Arpeggiata, *adagio andante e piano*

02 Cloud Level (Version 2), *piano molto e penseroso*

©2012, 2013, 2015, and 2020 Matthew Leigh Embleton

03 Eternal Recurrence (Version 2), *piano molto con affetuoso*

Matthew Leigh Embleton (b1978) Compositions for Recorder

Op 07 Journey in c-minor

01 Introduction, *andante*

©2012, 2013, 2015, and 2020 Matthew Leigh Embleton

Matthew Leigh Embleton (b1978) — Compositions for Recorder

02 Interlude, *adagio*

©2012, 2013, 2015, and 2020 Matthew Leigh Embleton

Matthew Leigh Embleton (b1978) — Compositions for Recorder

03 Conclusion, *allegro*

©2012, 2013, 2015, and 2020 Matthew Leigh Embleton

Matthew Leigh Embleton (b1978) — Compositions for Recorder

Op 08 Nocturne in c-minor

Piano molto e cantabile (Alto Recorder in F)

©2012, 2013, 2015, and 2020 Matthew Leigh Embleton

Matthew Leigh Embleton (b1978) Compositions for Recorder

Op 10 Extransience in d-minor

Affrettando con poco agitato

©2012, 2013, 2015, and 2020 Matthew Leigh Embleton

Matthew Leigh Embleton (b1978) Compositions for Recorder

Op 11 Victoria Park, December 2005 in e-minor (Version 2)

Piano molto e penseroso

©2012, 2013, 2015, and 2020 Matthew Leigh Embleton

Matthew Leigh Embleton (b1978) Compositions for Recorder

Op 12 Late Night Sky in g-minor

Piano molto e penseroso

©2012, 2013, 2015, and 2020 Matthew Leigh Embleton

Matthew Leigh Embleton (b1978) — Compositions for Recorder

©2012, 2013, 2015, and 2020 Matthew Leigh Embleton

Op 13 Introduction in g-minor

Piano molto e cantabile (Alto Recorder in F)

www.ingramcontent.com/pod-product-compliance
Lightning Source LLC
Chambersburg PA
CBHW051431070526
44584CB00023B/3684